A gift for:

_____

From:

_____

God Thinks You're Wonderful!

A collection of encouraging thoughts
from the published works of

Max Lucado

ILLUSTRATED BY CHRIS SHEA

MJF BOOKS
NEW YORK

Published by MJF Books
Fine Communications
322 Eighth Avenue
New York, NY 10001

God Thinks You're Wonderful!
LC Control Number 2008921872
ISBN-13: 978-1-56731-921-7
ISBN-10: 1-56731-921-1

Originally published by Thomas Nelson, Inc.®, Nashville, Tennessee 37214.
This edition is published by MJF Books in arrangement with Thomas Nelson, Inc.

Printed in Singapore.

MJF Books and the MJF colophon are trademarks of Fine Creative Media, Inc.

TWP   10   9   8   7   6   5   4   3

For Jack and Marsha Countryman.
God thinks you're wonderful,
and so do I.

MAX LUCADO

To my dad, Bill Givens,
with "such happiness."

CHRIS SHEA

God is fond of you . . .

If he had a wallet,

your photo would be in it.

If he had a refrigerator,
your picture would be on it.

He sends you flowers
every spring
and a sunrise
every morning.

good morning

Whenever

you want to talk,

he'll listen.

He can live anywhere

in the universe,

and he chose

your heart.

X — I AM here

Face it, friend.

He's crazy about you.

By the way,

it may be difficult

for you

to believe that

God knows your name . . .

but he does.

Written on his hand.

Spoken by his mouth.

Whispered by his lips.

Your name.

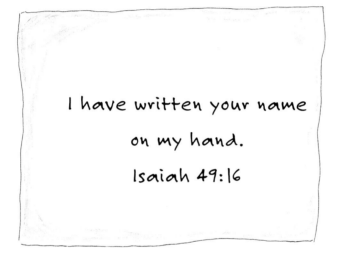
I have written your name
on my hand.
Isaiah 49:16

Blessings
Available

Peace

Love

Happiness

Parents

Kids

grand Kids

popcicles

Kittens

Sunsets

Carrots

Sun

moon

Stars

Pie

teachers

Friends

Storms

flowers

trees

dogs

intelligence

wonder

God

angels

Jesus

Try to
Place in →

Our hearts are
not large enough
to contain the blessings
that God wants to give.

So try this.

The next time a sunrise

steals your breath . . .

or a meadow of flowers

leaves you speechless . . .

remain that way.

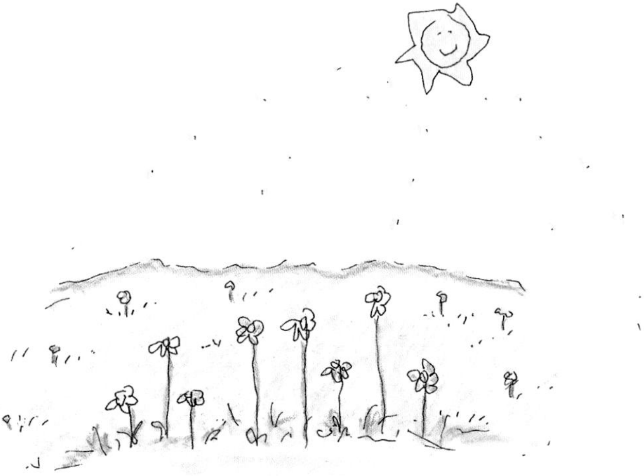

Say nothing and listen

as heaven whispers,

"Do you like it?

I did it just for you."

If we give gifts
to show our love,
how much more
would he?

He could have
left the world
flat and gray . . .
but he didn't.

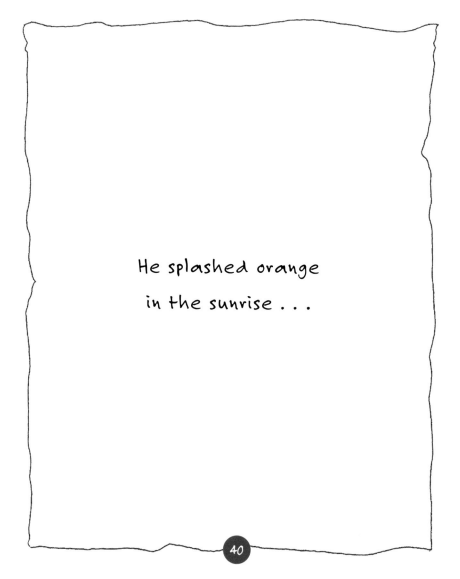

He splashed orange

in the sunrise . . .

and cast the sky

in blue.

And if you love

to see geese

as they gather,

chances are

you'll see that too.

Did he have to make

the squirrel's tail furry?

Was he obliged
to make the birds sing?

And the funny way
that chickens scurry . . .

or the majesty

of thunder

when it rings?

Why give a flower

fragrance?

Why give food
its taste?

Could it be

he loves to see

that look

upon your face?

So promise me
you'll never forget . . .
that you aren't
an accident
or an incident . . .
you are a gift
to the world,

a divine work of art,

signed by God.

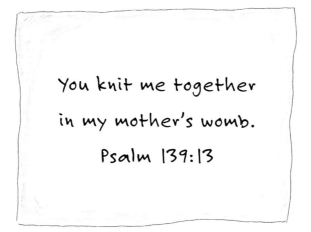

You knit me together in my mother's womb.

Psalm 139:13

You were

knit together.

You weren't
mass-produced.
You aren't an
assembly-line product.

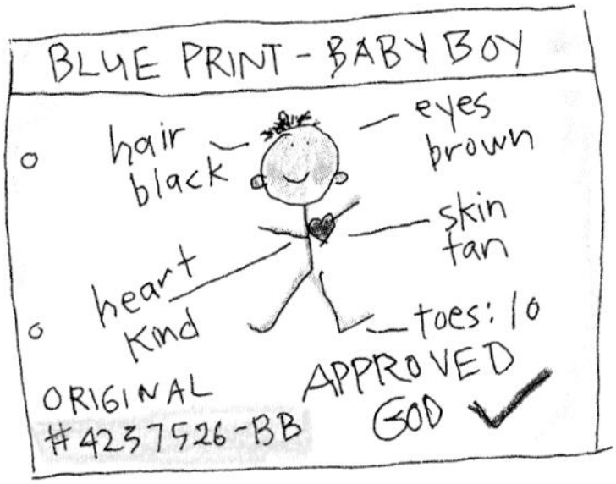
BLUE PRINT - BABY BOY
hair black
eyes brown
skin tan
heart kind
toes: 10
ORIGINAL
#4237526-BB
APPROVED
GOD

You were
deliberately planned,
specifically gifted,
and lovingly positioned
on this earth . . .

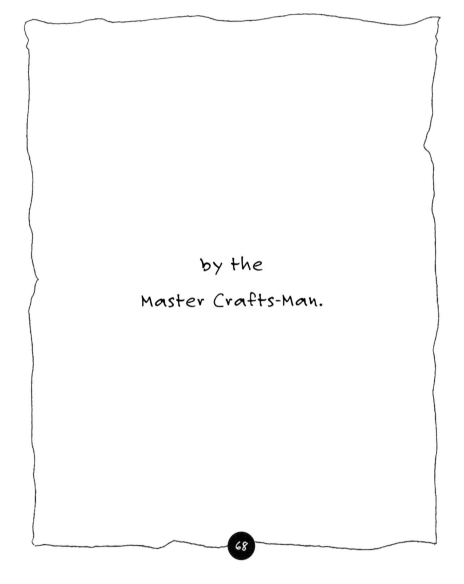

by the

Master Crafts-Man.

Bloom here!

He thinks you are
the best thing
to come down the pike
in quite a while.

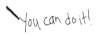

Turn to the sidelines;
that's God cheering
your run.

Look past the finish line;

that's God

applauding your steps.

God is for you.

Had he a calendar,

your birthday

would be circled.

If he drove a car,
your name would be
on his bumper.

If there's a tree in heaven,

he's carved your name

in the bark.

actual un-retouched photo

Maybe you don't want

to trouble God

with your hurts.

But . . .

"he cares about you"

(1 Peter 5:7).

He is waiting for you,

to embrace you

whether you

succeed or fail.

Your heavenly Father is
very fond of you
and only wants to share
his love with you.

Untethered by time,

God sees us all.

Vagabonds and ragamuffins all, he
saw us before we were born.
And he loves what he sees.

Flooded by emotion,

overcome by pride,

the Starmaker turns to us,

one by one, and says,

"You are my child.

I love you dearly.

I'm aware that
someday you'll turn from me
and walk away.

But I want you to know,

I've already provided

a way back."

You have captured

the heart of God.

He cannot bear to live

without you.

God's dream is
to make you right
with him.

Sins
Fault
Mistak

And the path to the cross

tells us exactly how far

God will go to call us back.

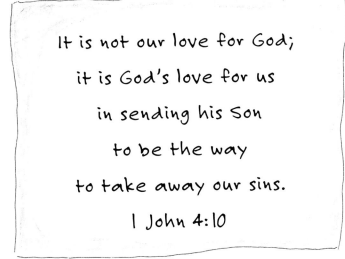

It is not our love for God;

it is God's love for us

in sending his Son

to be the way

to take away our sins.

1 John 4:10

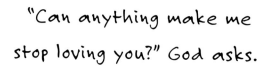

"Can anything make me stop loving you?" God asks.

"You wonder how long
my love will last?

Watch me speak your language,
sleep on your earth,
and feel your hurts.

Find your answer
on a splintered cross,
on a craggy hill.

That's how much

I love you."

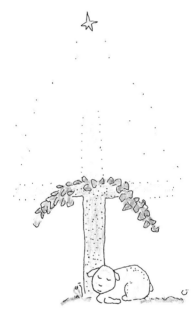

God does more
than forgive our mistakes;
he removes them!
We simply have
to take them to him.
You can talk to God
because God listens.

Let a tear appear

on your cheek, and

he is there to wipe it.

He has sent his angels

to care for you,

his Holy spirit

to dwell in you . . .

his church

to encourage you,

and his word

to guide you.

As much as you want
to see him, he wants
to see you more.

If you want

to touch God's heart,

use the name

he loves to hear.

Call him "Father."

He thinks

you're wonderful!